WELLES-TURNER MEMORIAL LIBRARY
GLASTONBURY, CT 06033

P9-DFO-392

DISCARDED BY
WELLES-TURNER
MEMORIAL LIBRARY
GLASTONBURY, CT

the best **fondue** cookbook

the best fondue cookbook

a beautiful collection of the world's most delicious fondues and dippers, from cheese and shrimp to delectable desserts, with 100 practical photographs

Becky Johnson

LORENZ BOOKS

This edition is published by Lorenz Books,
an imprint of Anness Publishing Ltd,
Hermes House, 88–89 Blackfriars Road,
London SE1 8HA
tel. 020 7401 2077; fax 020 7633 9499

www.lorenzbooks.com; www.annesspublishing.com

If you like the images in this book and would like to investigate using
them for publishing, promotions or advertising, please visit our website
www.practicalpictures.com for more information.

UK agent: The Manning Partnership Ltd;
tel. 01225 478444; fax 01225 478440;
sales@manning-partnership.co.uk
UK distributor: Grantham Book Services Ltd;
tel. 01476 541080; fax 01476 541061;
orders@gbs.tbs-ltd.co.uk
North American agent/distributor: National Book Network;
tel. 301 459 3366; fax 301 429 5746;
www.nbnbooks.com
Australian agent/distributor: Pan Macmillan Australia;
tel. 1300 135 113; fax 1300 135 103;
customer.service@macmillan.com.au
New Zealand agent/distributor: David Bateman Ltd;
tel. (09) 415 7664; fax (09) 415 8892

Publisher: Joanna Lorenz
Managing Editor: Linda Fraser
Editorial Reader: Joy Wotton
Production Controller: Joanna King
Indexer: Hilary Bird
Designer: Paul Oakley at Blue Banana
Photography: Tim Auty
Props Styling: Helen Trent
Food Styling: Becky Johnson

ETHICAL TRADING POLICY
Because of our ongoing ecological investment programme, you, as our customer, can have the
pleasure and reassurance of knowing that a tree is being cultivated on your behalf to naturally
replace the materials used to make the book you are holding. For further information about this
scheme, go to www.annesspublishing.com/trees

© Anness Publishing Limited 2002, 2008

All rights reserved. No part of this publication may be reproduced, stored in a retrieval system,
or transmitted in any way or by any means, electronic, mechanical, photocopying, recording
or otherwise, without the prior written permission of the copyright holder.

A CIP catalogue record for this book is available from the British Library.

Previously published as *Fondue*

NOTES
Bracketed terms are intended for American readers.
For all recipes, quantities are given in both metric and imperial measures and, where
appropriate, in standard cups and spoons. Follow one set of measures, but not a mixture,
because they are not interchangeable. Standard spoon and cup measures are level.
1 tsp = 5ml, 1 tbsp = 15ml, 1 cup = 250ml/8fl oz.
Australian standard tablespoons are 20ml. Australian readers should use 3 tsp in place
of 1 tbsp for measuring small quantities.
American pints are 16fl oz/2 cups. American readers should use 20fl oz/2.5 cups
in place of 1 pint when measuring liquids. Electric oven temperatures in this book are for
conventional ovens.
When using a fan oven, the temperature will probably need to be reduced by about
10–20°C/20–40°F. Since ovens vary, you should check with your manufacturer's instruction
book for guidance. Medium (US large) eggs are used unless otherwise stated.

Front cover shows Crème Anglaise with Raspberry Meringues – for recipe, see page 56.

Contents

Introduction

Fondues are hot – and that's not only their temperature. Their style is as funky as disco, as retro as shag-pile and as kitsch as a lava lamp. Long associated with swinging parties and flower-power hippies, they now embody the spirit of modern cooking: fast, simple, flexible and, above all, social. So, if you have yet to jump on the fondue revival bandwagon, now is your chance.

Below: Table-top cooking is perfect for this fondue version of a Mongolian firepot, where fresh vegetables and seafood are skewered on lemon grass sticks and then cooked in stock.

Above: Breadcrumbed fish goujons are ideal for cooking in an oil fondue as they take only a minute or two to cook.

In this book, the term fondue is loosely defined as any liquid that is kept hot at the table so that each diner can dip morsels of food into it. Included are recipes with smooth, melted cheese sauces; flavoursome stocks for cooking tasty titbits then drinking as a soup; and oil fondues where succulent meat, seafood and vegetables are crisply cooked before being dipped into mouthwatering sauces. Temptingly sweet fondues, with creamy or fruity sauces served with fruit or pastries, are also featured.

The recipes are all tried and tested and chosen from ideas gleaned from travels around the globe. They usually require some advance preparation, but this has been kept to a minimum. The real joy of the fondue becomes apparent once the diners are seated and everyone is able to participate in the cooking process. This takes some of the pressure away from the host and allows the diners to become involved in the shared, relaxed and fun experience that is the fondue.

The recipes begin with an old favourite: the creamy, traditional Swiss cheese fondue. Later in the book, other cuisines from around the world are represented: roasted tomato and mascarpone fondue with aubergine fritters from Italy, spiced Moroccan meatballs with harissa dip from North Africa and the aromatic, Thai-inspired tom yam.

Dessert fondues include a heavenly chocolate fondue with meltingly sweet poached pears and ice cream for dipping. If you prefer an exotic and fruity dessert, banana fritters with papaya cream or blackberry fondue with figs and frangipane pastries are guaranteed to fire up even the most jaded of palates.

Hopefully the ideas in this book will inspire you to invite friends and family to take part in this informal way of eating. So bring out the burners and the long forks and enjoy a return to the relaxed sociable dining, if not the heady, flower-power days, of the 1970s.

Above: Fresh blackberry purée is just one of the many sweet fondues, which range from smooth, creamy custard and rich chocolate sauce to papaya cream with deep-fried fritters for dipping.

Above: Big garlicky croûtes make a change from the cubes of bread that are traditionally dipped into a Swiss cheese fondue.

Equipment

It is not necessary to go out and purchase a fondue set if you want to host a fondue party, but you will need a few essentials.

Heat source

A small night light or candle is the simplest form of heat source that you could use, and this is perfectly sufficient for a chocolate fondue. However, it does not produce enough heat for either oil or stock fondues. For these you will need to use a special stainless steel burner. There are two types. One contains a sponge on to which an inflammable liquid, usually methylated spirits, is poured, and then ignited. The other comprises a small foil tray of gel-based fuel that simply slides into the burner and is discarded when used. A lid covers the burner, which can be adjusted to regulate the heat. Burners also have the advantage of being spill-proof so that any accidents are avoided. Electric fondue sets are available, which help to keep oil fondues up to temperature, but they do detract from the romance of a real flame.

Firepots

The Mongolian firepot incorporates a large, usually aluminium pot with a central funnel above a rack on to which burning coals or night lights are placed to heat the stock.

Above: Methylated spirit burners (left) and gel burners (top right) will create enough heat to cook both oil and stock fondues. Tiny night-light candles (bottom right) are only suitable for keeping sauces warm, but they are less likely to scorch delicate sauces like cheese or chocolate.

Right: The traditional aluminium Mongolian firepot is ideal for cooking stock-based fondues, but there's no need to go out and buy one specially as you can use a large pan, small wok or flameproof casserole instead.

Fondue sets

Inexpensive fondue sets are available that incorporate a pot, stand, forks and a burner. Cheaper sets with just a rack and burner can also be bought, as can individual pots and pans, forks and skewers.

Cutlery

Dinner forks can be used for dipping food into a fondue. However, when cooking food in the fondue, forks with handles are needed, as the metal of a fork or skewer will get dangerously hot when left in the fondue. Small wire baskets can be used to fish out food that has been deep-fried or cooked in stock. Chopsticks or small wooden tongs are the authentic equipment for cooking sukiyaki and tempura.

Above: Some fondue sets include a splashguard to protect diners' hands and support the forks while cooking.

Above: Fondue pots may have one or two handles. Pots with two handles are safer for oil and stock fondues.

Potholders or racks

Fondue stands comprise a rack, on which the pan or fondue pot is supported, and a base on which the burner or night light sits.

Fondue pots

It is not necessary to use a special fondue pot. Any pan, flameproof casserole or pot can sit on the rack as long as it is secure. Stainless steel is best for oil fondues, and any heavy-based pot for delicate cheese or sauce fondues.

Right: Dinner forks are fine for dipping foods into sauce fondues, but use special long-handled forks or skewers for cooking in stock or oil.

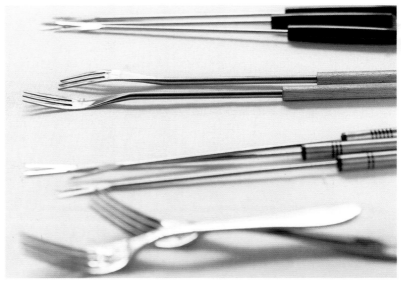

Techniques
and Guidelines

Fondues work best with small quantities, so don't invite too many guests – four or six people is about right. Check whether your fondue pot can be used on the stove, and if not prepare the fondue in a small pan and then transfer to the fondue pot. Ask diners to stir sauce fondues using a figure-of-eight motion with their dipping food, to keep the fondue creamy.

Below: *When dipping, stir the sauce in a figure of eight to keep it smooth.*

Cheese fondues

To add flavour, rub the inside of the fondue pot with the cut side of a garlic clove.

Grate or crumble cheese to help it melt quickly, and heat it gently as it burns easily.

The finished fondue should have a smooth and creamy consistency. If this is not the case, add a squeeze of lemon juice to help it bind together.

Stock fondues

Use a well-flavoured vegetable or chicken stock and don't over-fill the pan – it should be no more than two-thirds full. Add noodles or pasta to the stock, if you like, then serve as a soup once the food dippers have all been cooked.

Oil fondues

Use a cook's thermometer to check the oil temperature – it should be 190°C/375°F.

Alternatively, test the temperature by dropping a cube of day-old bread into the hot oil; it should brown in 30–60 seconds. If you transfer the oil from a pan to the fondue pot, place the fondue pot in the sink while you pour. Ensure that the pot is no more than two-thirds full.

Once the oil has been transferred to the table, adjust the burner to its highest setting (with all the air holes fully open). Don't cook too much food at one time as this will cool the oil and may cause it to froth up and overflow. You may need to reheat the oil on the stove if the temperature drops too much.

Sweet fondues

Custards, fruit purées and chocolate sauces can be cooked ahead of time and chilled until ready to reheat and serve. Cook custards gently as they may curdle and become grainy if overheated. If this should happen, plunge the base of the pan into a bowl of cold water to cool it quickly and add a little cold milk or cream, whisking rapidly.

Ensure that fruit sauces are thick enough to coat the food for dipping – if not, thicken with a little blended cornflour (cornstarch).

When melting chocolate, don't allow the bowl to get too hot, or the chocolate may overheat and "seize". Add liquids such as cream, coffee or liqueur before melting, and don't stir until the chocolate has melted completely.

Above: *A night-light candle is the best option for reheating delicate fondues, such as custard or chocolate, that scorch easily if overheated.*

SAFETY NOTES

- *If oil is overheated it could burst into flames. If it should catch light, place a lid or a damp dishtowel over the top of the pan very carefully to cut off the air supply – never pour water on to burning oil.*
- *Make sure that the food for dipping is dry, as wet food will cause the oil to spit.*

- *Protect your hands when moving a hot pan.*
- *Check that the fondue pot is secure on its stand on the table and that it cannot be knocked over accidentally.*
- *Never leave a lighted burner or candle unattended.*

Ingredients

The beauty of fondues is their simplicity: only a few ingredients are required to create an appealing and satisfying meal, but it is the imaginative combination of tastes that gives fondues their magic.

Above: *Soft cheeses such as goat's cheese are usually melted in milk rather than lemon juice or alcohol.*

Cheese

The classic cheese fondues use mild-flavoured cheeses from Switzerland, such as Emmenthal, Gruyère and Appenzeller, which have an elastic texture when melted. They need to be cooked with acidic wines, liqueurs or lemon juice to help produce a smooth fondue. Other suitable cheeses include Beaufort, mozzarella, Edam, Fontina and Cheddar; try them for their subtle differences of taste and texture.

For the lighter, less alcoholic soft-cheese fondues, choose strong to mild-flavoured goat's cheeses or very mild but tangy soft cheeses

Above: *Hard cheeses should be teamed with dry, acidic wines, such as Zinfandel or Swiss Chasselas.*

such as herb or pepper-flavoured cream cheese, ricotta or mascarpone. The strong tastes of blue cheeses are also excellent, from the creamy Dolcelatte, Bleu d'Auvergne and Gorgonzola to the more pungent and crumblier Stilton. These cheeses are melted in milk instead of alcohol or lemon juice.

Alcohol

Use a dry and acidic wine with hard cheeses. A good choice is Swiss Chasselas or any full-flavoured, dry white wine.

For a fruity flavour try cider, or, if you are using a good, mature, British hard cheese, a real-ale beer makes a full-flavoured fondue.

Right: *Firm cheeses such as Gruyère and Emmenthal need to be cooked with wine, liqueur or lemon juice.*

Liqueurs add flavour and ensure a smooth cheese fondue – Kirsch is a favourite. Enhance a chocolate fondue with the orange flavour of Cointreau or Grand Marnier, or use coffee Kahlúa or almond-flavoured Disaronno Amaretto. Fruit liqueurs will transform fruit-purée fondues, adding a rich flavour.

Oil

Light-coloured and mild-flavoured oils, which can be heated to high temperatures without smoking, are best for oil fondues. Choose from vegetable, corn, sunflower, groundnut (peanut) or soya oils. Olive, sesame and nut oils are too strongly flavoured to be suitable and are inclined to burn at high temperatures. If you enjoy the flavour of these oils, add one or two spoonfuls to one of the milder oils.

Below: Choose mild-flavoured oils such as vegetable and sunflower for oil fondues.

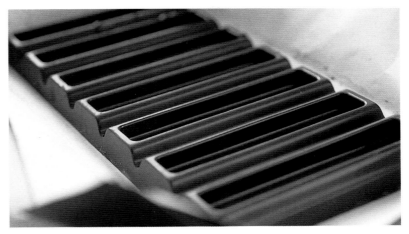

Above: Good quality, strongly flavoured chocolate with a high proportion of cocoa solids is best for fondues.

Chocolate

The most expensive chocolates are usually the best for a fondue, as they contain a larger proportion of cocoa solids, sometimes as much as 90 per cent compared to 17 per cent in a cheaper variety. These good quality dark chocolates are also known as bitter chocolate; they contain very little cream or vegetable fat and no sugar. You will need to use less than the cheaper alternatives to achieve a good taste. Try organic Green & Black's cooking chocolate or Valrhona chocolate. Even when cream and sugar are added to a chocolate fondue, the rich flavour of the chocolate will remain. For a sweeter and milder fondue use good quality milk or white chocolate. Don't use chocolate cake covering for a fondue – the flavour simply isn't good enough.

Whatever the chocolate you choose, melt it carefully in a bowl over a pan of hot, but not boiling, water and don't allow it to overheat.

Simple Dippers

A selection of natural and ready-made foods make ideal dippers for a fondue, with little or no preparation. These dippers can often be hand-held, but some may need to be speared on to long-handled fondue forks.

Above and right: Breadsticks make great dippers, as do gherkins, tortilla chips and olives.

Bread, crisps and crackers

Choose bread with different textures: French sticks, bagels, sourdough and soda breads, seeded breads, such as Spanish Gallego or poppy-seed-crusted breads, and nut breads. Also try Italian breads, such as sun-dried tomato, onion or olive focaccia and ciabatta.

Right: Croûtons make tasty bitesize dippers, but slices of fresh bread are equally good.

If you can, match the bread to the cheese: a Dolcelatte fondue will pair perfectly with sun-dried tomato and olive focaccia, for example. The bread can be cubed or sliced and eaten fresh, grilled, toasted or fried in a little butter and oil until crisp.

Crisps (US potato chips) and crackers also make simple dippers for cheese fondues. Try corn chips, breadsticks – plain or wrapped in prosciutto – or cheese straws. Make sure that they are large enough to be hand-held while dipped into the fondue, and that they will not disintegrate once laden with the sauce.

For sweet fondues, cubes or slices of sweet breads such as croissants and brioche make good dippers.

Fruit

Some fruits, such as grapes and apples, are suitable for dipping into savoury as well as sweet fondues. Take advantage of fruits in season for sweet fondues: strawberries, cherries, plums, peaches, apricots and nectarines are all suitable, as well as exotic fruits such as figs, pineapple, papaya, mangoes, star fruit and lychees. Fruits available all year, such as bananas and the citrus fruits, also dip well. Underripe fruit can be lightly poached in sugar syrup, fruit juice or a fruity wine; this works especially well for pears.

Cakes, biscuits and cookies

Slices of dense-textured cake and sweet biscuits or cookies make excellent dippers for sweet fondues. Try Madeira cake, meringues, biscotti, Danish pastries or chocolate-chip cookies – whatever you fancy.

Vegetables

Fresh, raw vegetable dippers, prepared as crudités, add a light crunch to a cheese fondue. Choose from pink radishes, baby carrots, baby corn, sugar snap peas or mangetouts (snow peas), red, orange and yellow (bell) peppers, young celery, chicory (Belgian endive), cucumber and fennel. Some vegetables, such as asparagus spears, cauliflower or broccoli florets, baby leeks and green beans, are best lightly blanched in salted boiling water until they are lightly cooked, but still retain their crunch.

Above: Crunchy, fresh vegetables perfectly complement a creamy cheese fondue, while biscotti, small fruits and cakes (top left) are wonderful with sweet fondues.

Left: For chocolate fondues, small cubes of firm-textured cakes go well with a selection of exotic fruits.

Cheese
fondues

Creamy sauces made from melted cheese make delectable dips for all kinds of foods. Try rich and flavourful Dolcelatte fonduta, mild roasted tomato and mascarpone fondue or goat's cheese fondue.

Serves 4–6

2 French batons or 1 baguette

1–2 garlic cloves, halved

1 small head broccoli, divided
into florets

1 small head cauliflower, divided
into florets

200g/7oz mangetouts
(snow peas) or green
beans, trimmed

115g/4oz baby carrots,
trimmed, or 2 medium
carrots, cut into long wedges

250ml/8fl oz/1 cup dry
white wine

115g/4oz/1 cup grated
Gruyère cheese

250g/9oz/2¼ cups grated
Emmenthal cheese

15ml/1 tbsp cornflour
(cornstarch)

30ml/2 tbsp Kirsch

freshly grated nutmeg

salt and ground black pepper

For the dressing

30ml/2 tbsp extra virgin
olive oil

rind and juice of 2 lemons

25g/1oz/½ cup chopped
fresh parsley

25g/1oz/½ cup chopped
fresh mint

1 red chilli, seeded and
finely chopped

This classic, richly flavoured fondue is traditionally served with cubes of bread, but here it's updated with herby vegetable dippers and garlic toasts.

Swiss Cheese
Fondue with Warm, Herbed Vegetables and Garlic Croûtes

Cut the French batons or baguette on the diagonal into 1cm/½in slices, then toast on both sides. Rub one side of each toasted slice with the cut side of a garlic clove, if you like, and transfer to a serving platter.

Blanch all the vegetables for two minutes in a large pan of salted boiling water, then place them in a large bowl. While they are hot, add all the dressing ingredients, season, and toss together.

Rub the inside of the fondue pot with the cut side of a garlic clove. Pour in the wine and heat gently on the stove. Gradually add the grated cheeses, stirring constantly until melted. Mix the cornflour with the Kirsch and add, then stir until thickened.

Season with salt, pepper and grated nutmeg to taste. When the fondue is hot and smooth, but not boiling, transfer to a burner at the table.

Each diner dips the vegetables and toasted bread into the fondue.

INGREDIENTS

Serves 6

*225g/8oz/1 cup Greek
  (US strained plain) yogurt*
150ml/¼ pint/⅔ cup milk
450g/1lb feta cheese, crumbled
*15ml/1 tbsp cornflour
  (cornstarch)*
*500g/1¼lb watermelon, cut
  into 6 wedges*
salt and ground black pepper
*warmed pitta bread, Greek
  marinated olives and salad,
  to serve*

For the spicy sardines

45ml/3 tbsp olive oil
2 shallots, finely chopped
3 garlic cloves, crushed
*1 red chilli, seeded and
  finely chopped*
*small bunch coriander (cilantro)
  or flat leaf parsley,
  finely chopped*
*12 fresh sardines, cleaned and
  backbones removed*
juice of 1 lemon

Conjure up memories of relaxing holidays on hot, sunny Greek islands with this mezze-inspired dish. Salty olives, chilli-spiced sardines and fresh watermelon make perfect partners for this creamy yogurt and feta fondue.

Feta Fondue with Spicy
Sardines and Watermelon

Soak 12 cocktail sticks (toothpicks) in cold water for 30 minutes. Prepare the spicy sardines. Heat 15ml/1 tbsp of the oil in a frying pan and add the shallots and garlic. Cook for a few minutes, then add the chilli and coriander or parsley. Spread the onion mixture over the flesh-side of the sardines, roll them up from the head to the tail and secure with a cocktail stick.

Gently heat the yogurt and milk together until hot but not boiling, then add the cheese and stir until smooth. Blend the cornflour with 30ml/2 tbsp of water and stir into the cheese mixture. Season. Cook gently until thickened, then transfer to a fondue pot and place on a burner at the table.

To cook the sardines, heat the remaining olive oil in a frying pan and fry the sardines for 3–4 minutes. Add the lemon juice and transfer to a serving platter. Diners dip the sardines into the fondue. Serve the fondue with chunky watermelon wedges, warm pitta bread, olives and salad.

INGREDIENTS

Serves 4–6

250ml/8fl oz/1 cup milk
*6 thyme sprigs, woody stems
   removed, chopped, plus extra
   thyme leaves for garnishing*
*200g/7oz/scant 1 cup light
   cream cheese*
*115g/4oz/1/2 cup young, soft
   goat's cheese*
*15ml/1 tbsp cornflour
   (cornstarch)*
salt and ground black pepper

For the potatoes
*450g/1lb streaky (fatty) bacon
   rashers (strips)*
*1kg/2¹/₄lb small new
   potatoes, scrubbed*
24 small bay leaves

VARIATIONS

• *Use fresh parsley instead of
thyme, if you prefer.*
• *Try Italian pancetta instead
of the bacon and wrap each
potato with one or two fresh
basil leaves in place of the bay.*

**Bay-scented baby potatoes wrapped
with thin strips of bacon and then
dipped into tangy melting goat's
cheese make a sublime mouthful.**

Goat's Cheese and Thyme Fondue with Crispy Bacon Baked Potatoes

First, prepare the potatoes. Preheat the oven to 200°/400°F/Gas 6. Stretch each bacon rasher with the back of a knife, then slice in half across the middle. Wrap each of the potatoes and a bay leaf in a piece of bacon and then place them join side down in a baking tray. Season with pepper and bake for 30–35 minutes, or until the potatoes are tender and the bacon is crisp.

Meanwhile, heat all but 30ml/2 tbsp of the milk with the thyme until hot but not boiling. Add the cream cheese and the goat's cheese, then beat or whisk the mixture until it is smooth.

Blend the cornflour to a paste with the remaining milk, then add to the fondue and stir until thick. Season with salt and pepper, then transfer to a fondue pot, scatter a little extra thyme on top of the fondue mixture and place on a burner at the table.

Serve the hot, bacon-wrapped potatoes for dipping into the fondue. You can either eat the crisp bay leaves, or remove them.

INGREDIENTS

Serves 4

*450ml/³⁄₄ pint/scant 2 cups
    milk*

*200g/7oz Dolcelatte cheese,
    diced*

*115g/4oz/1 cup grated
    mozzarella cheese*

*15ml/1 tbsp cornflour
    (cornstarch)*

60ml/4 tbsp dry white wine

salt and ground black pepper

For the rosemary skewers

*12 woody rosemary stems,
    about 15cm/6in long*

*12 slices prosciutto, sliced in
    half lengthways*

*400g/14oz walnut bread loaf,
    cut into large cubes*

12 ready-to-eat prunes, pitted

*2 courgettes (zucchini), halved
    lengthways and cut into
    1cm/¹⁄₂ in slices*

25g/1oz/2 tbsp butter

30ml/2 tbsp olive oil

1 garlic clove, crushed

VARIATIONS

*The rosemary sticks could be
threaded with a variety of
quick-cooking foods, from
pieces of sausage to firm fish
such as salmon or cod, and
vegetables, such as mushrooms
or cherry tomatoes.*

Fonduta is the Italian version of the fondue, and it is usually made from mixtures of Fontina, Provolone or Gorgonzola cheeses. For this recipe, creamy Dolcelatte cheese is mixed with the lighter mozzarella.

Dolcelatte Fonduta
with Rosemary Skewers

Remove all but the top leaves from the rosemary stems and soak them in cold water for 30 minutes. Gently heat the milk on the stove in a fondue pot, then add the cheeses and stir until smooth. Season well.

Blend the cornflour with the wine, add to the cheese mixture and stir until thickened.

Meanwhile, prepare the rosemary skewers. Take a soaked rosemary skewer and thread on one end of a piece of prosciutto. Add a bread

cube, a prune and one or two slices of courgette, interleaving the proscuitto between the ingredients, so that the prosciutto is speared several times. Repeat with the other rosemary sticks.

Heat the butter with the oil in a large frying pan and gently fry the garlic for a few minutes. Add the skewers to the frying pan and cook for a minute on each side until hot and golden brown.

Place the fondue pot on a burner at the table. Diners remove the vegetables from the skewers and use fondue forks to dip the vegetables into the hot fondue.

INGREDIENTS

Serves 4–6

1kg/2¼lb very ripe tomatoes,
   on the vine
45ml/3 tbsp olive oil, plus extra
   for shallow frying
1 large onion,
   finely chopped
2 garlic cloves, crushed
30ml/2 tbsp Worcestershire
   sauce
5ml/1 tsp brown sugar
250g/9oz/generous 1 cup
   mascarpone cheese
small bunch basil or flat leaf
   parsley, torn or chopped
salt and ground black pepper

For the fritters

18 baby aubergines (eggplant),
   sliced in half lengthways, or
   2 medium aubergines, each
   cut into 1cm/½in thick
   slices then halved to make
   half-moon shapes
190g/6¾oz jar pesto
200g/7oz/scant 1 cup polenta
   valsugana (pre-cooked
   maize meal)

VARIATION

*For a change, replace the plain
pesto with red pepper pesto, a
fresh coriander (cilantro) pesto,
olive paste or, for a fiery touch,
add a little harissa.*

A piquant and creamy tomato sauce is heavenly for dipping crisp polenta and pesto aubergine fritters. Use very ripe tomatoes for the best flavour.

Roasted Tomato and Mascarpone Fondue with Aubergine Fritters

Preheat the oven to 200°C/400°F/Gas 6. Place the tomatoes in a roasting pan, season with salt and pepper and drizzle over 30ml/2 tbsp of the oil. Roast for 20 minutes.

Meanwhile, heat the remaining oil in a large frying pan and sauté the onion and garlic over a low heat for about 10 minutes, or until softened, but not browned. Remove the skins from the roasted tomatoes, then add to the pan with the Worcestershire sauce, sugar and a little more seasoning, and cook for 15–20 minutes, breaking up the tomatoes with a wooden spoon.

To make the fritters, spread the cut sides of the aubergine with a little pesto. Put the polenta on a plate and press the pesto-coated aubergines into it. Heat the oil for frying in a large frying pan and fry the aubergines in batches for 3–4 minutes on each side.

Stir the mascarpone and basil or parsley into the tomato sauce. Transfer to a fondue pot and place on a burner at the table. Serve with the fritters for dipping.

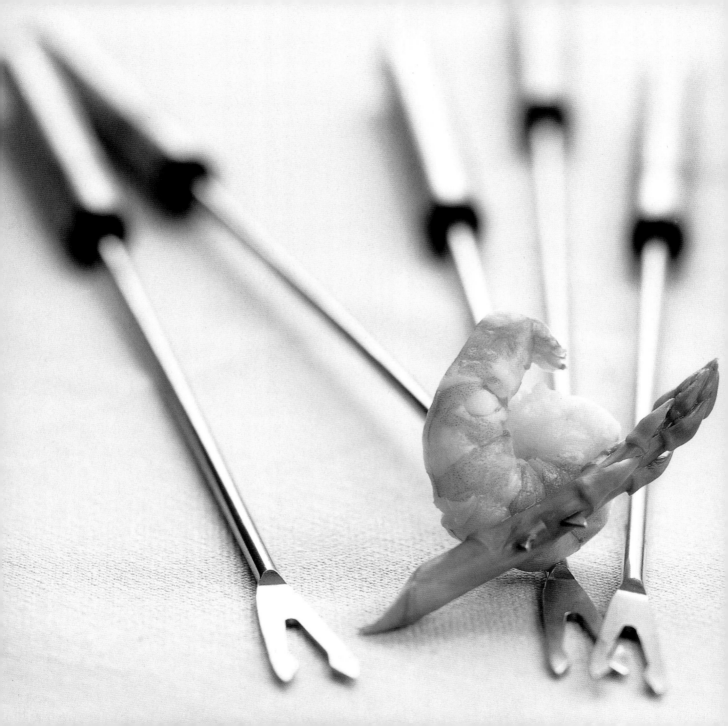

Stock
fondues

In these unusual fondues, guests cook bitesize portions of fish, small shellfish, morsels of meat, vegetables and tofu and even stuffed pasta in flavoursome, simmering stocks at the table.

INGREDIENTS

Serves 4–6

8–12 whole raw tiger or king
    prawns (jumbo shrimp), peeled
    and deveined, with tails on
2 skinless salmon or tuna fillets,
    about 150g/5oz each
6 sachets instant miso soup mixed
    with 1.75 litres/3 pints/7¹/2 cups
    water or the same quantity of
    fish, chicken or vegetable stock
handful of coriander (cilantro) leaves
2–3 spring onions (scallions), sliced
small bunch watercress, rocket
    (arugula) or young mizuma greens
50g/2oz enoki mushrooms
200g/7oz fine egg noodles
8–12 lemon grass stalks or
    wooden skewers
soy sauce and wasabi paste or
    horseradish sauce, to serve

For the marinade

rind and juice of 2 limes
15ml/2 tbsp soy sauce
2.5cm/1in piece fresh root ginger,
    peeled and finely chopped
2 garlic cloves, finely chopped
15ml/1 tbsp clear honey
1 red chilli, seeded and chopped

COOK'S TIP

To make them easier to eat,
snip the noodles into short
lengths using a pair of scissors.

In this easy-to-prepare fondue, pretty pink prawn tails and cubes of fish are marinated with garlic, ginger and chilli, then skewered with fragrant lemon grass stalks before being cooked at the table in a flavourful stock.

Mongolian Firepot

Wash the prawns, pat dry and place in a deep serving bowl. Cut the salmon or tuna fillets into 2.5cm/1in cubes and add to the prawns.

Mix all the marinade ingredients together and add to the bowl of seafood. Toss gently to coat, then cover and leave the seafood to marinate in the refrigerator for a minimum of 10 minutes, or 2 hours if possible.

Pour the stock into a pan, add the coriander and spring onions and bring to the boil. Transfer to a fondue pot and place on a burner at the table or pour the stock into a firepot at the table and keep hot.

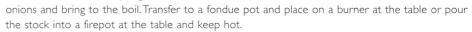

Arrange the salad leaves and mushrooms on serving plates, and put the soy sauce and wasabi or horseradish into small bowls. Add the noodles to the stock at the table and leave to cook.

Invite each diner to spear a cube of fish or a prawn on to a lemon grass stalk or skewer with a salad leaf and a mushroom. This is then submerged in the stock for 1 minute, or until the fish or prawn is cooked, then dipped into the soy sauce and wasabi or horseradish. When the fish and vegetables are all eaten, divide the remaining stock and noodles among soup bowls to eat.

INGREDIENTS

Serves 4–6

*450g/1lb fillet steak (beef
    tenderloin)*
*250g/9oz tofu, cut into
    1cm/¹/2in cubes*
*200g/7oz sugar snap peas or
    green beans sliced diagonally
    in half*
*1 bunch purple spring onions
    (scallions), sliced diagonally
    into 2.5cm/1in pieces*
juice of 1 lime
*small bunch of coriander
    (cilantro), chopped*
*lime wedges and boiled jasmine
    and wild rice, to serve*

For the marinade

*2.5cm/1in piece fresh
    root ginger, peeled and
    finely chopped*
1 garlic clove, crushed
*15ml/1 tbsp wholegrain
    mustard*
60ml/4 tbsp soy sauce
15ml/1 tbsp sesame oil

For the warishita stock

30ml/2 tbsp brown sugar
*45ml/3 tbsp mirin or
    sweet sherry*
*100ml/3¹/2fl oz/scant ¹/2 cup
    soy sauce*
*100ml/3¹/2fl oz/scant ¹/2 cup
    vegetable stock*

Thin slices of tender, marinated beef, tofu and vegetables are fried and then simmered in a sweet stock at the table in this Japanese dish. They are then dipped in a delicious ginger and mustard marinade before they are eaten.

Sukiyaki

Place the fillet steak between two pieces of baking parchment and beat out with a meat bat or rolling pin until thin. Cut into 2.5cm/1in wide, bitesize strips.

Place all the marinade ingredients in a large dish, add the beef and tofu and toss together until well coated. Set aside. Mix the warishita stock ingredients together in a bowl or jug (pitcher).

Heat a small wok or frying pan until very hot, then transfer to a burner at the table. Add the marinated beef and tofu to the hot wok and cook for a few seconds on each side, turning with tongs or long chopsticks. Add the warishita stock and the vegetables to the wok or pan and cook for a few minutes, or until tender, then add the lime juice and coriander. Spoon the marinade into individual dipping saucers.

Diners help themselves from the wok with their chopsticks and eat the sukiyaki dipped in the marinade and served with lime wedges and bowls of jasmine and wild rice.

VARIATION

Sukiyaki can also be made using venison or tuna steaks in place of the fillet steak.

INGREDIENTS

Serves 4–6

*200g/7oz raw tiger prawns
   (shrimp), peeled and deveined*
*350g/12oz cod fillet, or other firm
   white fish, skin removed*
*1 bunch spring onions
   (scallions), chopped*
*2 kaffir lime leaves,
   finely chopped*
*1 lemon grass stalk,
   finely chopped*
15ml/1 tbsp soy sauce
*30ml/2 tbsp cornflour
   (cornstarch)*
*1.5 litres/2¹/2 pints/6¹/4 cups
   instant miso soup or
   chicken stock*
*200g/7oz cellophane noodles,
   soaked in cold water*
*small bunch coriander (cilantro),
   chopped, to garnish*

For the marinated baby corn

*1 red chilli, seeded and
   finely chopped*
*1cm/¹/2in fresh root ginger, peeled
   and grated*
5ml/1 tsp honey
5ml/1 tsp rice wine vinegar
5ml/1 tsp sesame oil
*15ml/1 tbsp chopped fresh
   coriander (cilantro)*
130g/4¹/2oz baby corn

This unique Thai dish combines hot, sour, savoury and sweet flavours. Small prawn balls scented with lemon grass and kaffir lime leaves are cooked in an aromatic stock and eaten with sweet, crunchy, marinated baby corn.

Tom Yam Soup

Rinse the prawns and pat dry. Remove any bones from the white fish. Place the prawns, fish, spring onions, kaffir lime leaves, lemon grass and soy sauce in a food processor or blender and blend to a rough paste. Roll into cherry-tomato-size balls, dust lightly with cornflour, then place in a single layer on a serving platter and chill until required.

To make the marinated baby corn, mix the chilli, ginger, honey, rice wine vinegar, oil and chopped coriander in a serving bowl, add the baby corn and leave to marinate for 1–2 hours.

Bring the stock to the boil in a fondue pot. Snip the noodles into short lengths with scissors, and add to the stock with the coriander. Transfer to a burner at the table.

Diners help themselves to the prawn balls, dropping them into the hot stock for a minute or so, until pink and cooked through. Serve with the marinated baby corn, skewering these on to cocktail sticks (toothpicks) to make them easy to hold.

When all the prawn balls are cooked and eaten, ladle the stock with the noodles into individual warmed soup bowls to eat.

INGREDIENTS

Serves 4

1 chicken, about 2.25kg/5lb

1 parsley sprig

15ml/1 tbsp black peppercorns

1 bay leaf

300g/11oz baby carrots

175g/6oz baby leeks

25g/1oz/2 tbsp butter

15ml/1 tbsp olive oil

300g/11oz shallots, halved
   if large

200ml/7fl oz/scant 1 cup dry
   white wine

800g/13/4lb baby new potatoes

120ml/4fl oz/1/2 cup double
   (heavy) cream

salt and ground black pepper

small bunch parsley or tarragon,
   chopped, to garnish

In France, a pot au feu traditionally contains beef simmered in a rich stock, although chicken is also used. In this recipe, a lovely wine and herb-scented stock contains tender morsels of chicken and spring vegetables.

Chicken Pot au Feu

Joint the chicken into eight pieces and place the carcass in a large stockpot. Add the parsley sprig, peppercorns, bay leaf and the trimmings from the carrots and leeks. Cover with cold water and bring to the boil. Simmer for 45 minutes, then strain. Meanwhile, melt the butter with the olive oil in a frying pan, then add the chicken pieces, season, and brown all over. Lift out the chicken pieces on to a plate and add the shallots to the pan. Cook over a low heat for 20 minutes, stirring occasionally, until softened, but not browned.

Return the chicken to the pan and add the wine. Scrape up any juices from the bottom of the pan with a wooden spoon, then add the carrots, leeks and potatoes with enough of the stock to just cover. Bring to the boil, then cover and simmer for 20 minutes. Stir in the cream.

Transfer to a fondue pot and place on a burner at the table. Diners help themselves, sprinkling over the herbs.

COOK'S TIPS

• Any leftover stock can be kept in the refrigerator and used in other recipes.

• You could use large potatoes, but they will need to be par-boiled first so that they will cook in 10–15 minutes in the pot with the other ingredients.

INGREDIENTS

Serves 4–6

675g/1¹/₂lb butternut squash
115g/4oz/1¹/₃ cups freshly
 grated Parmesan cheese
1 bunch parsley, finely chopped
50g/2oz/¹/₂ cup pine
 nuts, toasted
500g/1¹/₄lb fresh lasagne
 sheets
1 egg, beaten
900ml/1¹/₂ pints/3³/₄ cups
 fresh chicken stock
salt and ground black pepper

For the sauce

50g/2oz/¹/₃ cup walnut pieces
5 ready-to-eat dried apricots,
 roughly chopped
2 slices wholemeal
 (whole-wheat) bread
250g/9oz/generous 1 cup
 ricotta cheese
75ml/2¹/₂fl oz/¹/₃ cup milk

COOK'S TIP

To toast pine nuts, spread them in a grill (broiling) pan and heat under a hot grill for 2 minutes. Stir or shake the pan frequently to prevent them from burning. Alternatively, put them in a pan and dry-fry them briefly, until they turn golden in colour and give off a wonderful aroma.

The perfect Italian-inspired recipe for cooking at the table – little ravioli pillows cooked in a tasty broth and served with a superb creamy nut sauce.

Walnut Sauce
with Butternut Squash Ravioli

Preheat the oven to 200°C/400°F/Gas 6. Bake the squash on a baking tray for 45 minutes.

Cut the baked squash in half lengthways, remove the seeds and scoop out the flesh. Put the flesh into a food processor with the grated Parmesan cheese, half the parsley, the pine nuts and seasoning, and blend to a rough purée.

Using a 6cm/2½in fluted pastry (cookie) cutter, cut out two rounds from each lasagne sheet. Put 5ml/1 tsp of the squash mixture into the centre of half the rounds, then brush the edges of each one with a little beaten egg. Place a second round on top of each one, then pinch together the edges to make ravioli. Transfer to a serving platter.

To make the sauce, place the walnuts, apricots, bread and remaining parsley in a food processor or blender and process to fairly fine crumbs. Add the ricotta cheese and pulse to mix. Spoon into

a pan, add the milk, then heat gently, stirring constantly until smooth. Pour the sauce into a warmed serving jug (pitcher).

Heat the stock in a fondue pot to boiling point, and then place on a burner at the table.

Invite diners to drop their own ravioli into the stock for 2–3 minutes. When cooked, fish them out with wire baskets, long-handled forks or tongs, and eat with the warm walnut sauce.

Oil
fondues

In these fondues, delicious tit-bits, quickly fried at the table, are served with flavourful sauces for dipping. Try crab cakes with Thai relish, crisp fish goujons with guacamole or Japanese tempura.

INGREDIENTS

Serves 4–6

450g/1lb sole or pink
   trout fillets
115g/4oz/1 cup plain
   (all-purpose) flour
10ml/2 tsp chilli powder
2 eggs, beaten
200g/7oz/3 1/2 cups fresh
   breadcrumbs
oil, for deep-frying
salt and ground black pepper
4–6 soft wheat tortillas, cut
   into wedges
lime wedges, to serve

For the guacamole

4 large ripe avocados
juice and thinly pared and
   shredded rind of 2 limes
1 garlic clove, crushed
200ml/7fl oz/scant 1 cup
   crème fraîche
2 spring onions (scallions),
   finely chopped

COOK'S TIP

*A Mexican trick of pushing the
avocado stone (pit) back into
the centre of the prepared
guacamole and then covering it
tightly with clear film (plastic
wrap) prevents the guacamole
from discolouring. Remove the
stone before serving.*

Small pieces of sole or trout are given a spicy coating, with a hint of chilli, and crisply fried at the table. They are served with an extra-creamy version of guacamole in this tasty combination of French and Mexican cuisine.

Chilli-crusted Goujons
with Guacamole and Tortillas

Cut the fish fillets on the diagonal into pieces about 5mm/¼in thick and 6cm/2½in long. Mix the flour with the chilli powder and salt on a plate. Put the eggs into a shallow bowl. Dip the fish first in the chilli flour, then the egg and finally the breadcrumbs. Place on a serving platter and chill.

To make the guacamole, cut the avocados in half and remove the stones (pits), then scoop out the flesh and mash with the lime juice, garlic, crème fraîche and spring onions. Season with salt and pepper. Put into a serving bowl, garnish with the lime shreds, and chill until ready to serve.

Heat the oil in a wok or pan to 190°C/375°F, or test by dropping a cube of day-old bread into the hot oil; it should brown in 30–60 seconds. Place the wok or pan on a burner at the table.

Invite each diner to drop the goujons into the hot oil for 2 minutes, or until golden. Deep-fry the tortilla pieces for a few seconds. Remove with tongs. Eat with the guacamole accompanied by lime wedges for squeezing.

INGREDIENTS

Serves 4–6

10ml/2 tsp chilli flakes
15ml/1 tbsp cumin seeds
1cm/1/2in piece of cinnamon stick
5ml/1 tsp mustard seeds
5ml/1 tsp ground turmeric
400g/14oz can chickpeas,
   drained
400g/14oz minced
   (ground) meat
1 large onion, finely chopped
2 large garlic cloves, crushed
1 egg
15ml/1 tbsp Worcestershire
   sauce
30ml/2 tbsp tomato
   purée (paste)
small bunch parsley, chopped
salt and ground black pepper
oil, for deep-frying

For the harissa dip

225g/8oz/1 cup thick Greek (US
   strained plain) yogurt
25ml/1 1/2 tbsp rose water
10ml/2 tsp harissa

COOK'S TIPS

- *Lamb, beef or chicken can be used for the meatballs.*
- *If you'd prefer to make them vegetarian, use vegetarian mince or Quorn and omit the Worcestershire sauce.*

Harissa is a hot and spicy chilli sauce, which makes a delicious dip when mixed with rose water and yogurt. It is the perfect accompaniment for these dainty and spicy meatballs, which are cooked at the table in a few minutes.

Spiced Moroccan
Meatballs with Harissa Dip

Grind the chilli, cumin, cinnamon, mustard seeds and turmeric together in a mortar and pestle.

Place the chickpeas in a food processor and process them to a pulp. Transfer to a large bowl and add the minced meat, onion, garlic, egg, Worcestershire sauce, tomato purée and parsley. Add the ground spices and season with salt and pepper. Mix together well.

Take small amounts of the mixture and shape into balls the size of cherry tomatoes. You should have about 60 balls. Place the spicy meatballs on a serving platter, and chill until ready to eat.

To make the harissa dip, stir together the yogurt, rose water and harissa and chill.

Heat the oil for deep-frying in a wok or deep pan to 190°C/375°F. If you do not have a cook's thermometer test by dropping in a cube of day-old bread; it should brown in 30–60 seconds. Carefully transfer the wok or pan to a burner at the table.

Diners cook the meatballs for 3–5 minutes, then dunk them in the harissa dip.

INGREDIENTS

Serves 4–6

25g/1oz cellophane noodles

250g/9oz minced (ground) pork

1 bunch spring onions
    (scallions), finely chopped

200g/7oz beansprouts

small bunch coriander
    (cilantro), chopped

15ml/1 tbsp soy sauce

5ml/1 tsp Thai fish sauce

5ml/1 tsp brown sugar

250g/9oz pack small spring
    roll wrappers (12cm/4^1/2in
    square)

15ml/1 tbsp plain (all-purpose)
    flour mixed with
    15ml/1 tbsp water

vegetable oil, for deep-frying

coriander (cilantro) sprigs and
    lettuce leaves to serve

For the satay sauce

1 small fresh chilli, seeded

1 garlic clove, finely chopped

15ml/1 tbsp vegetable oil

400ml/14fl oz can coconut milk

30ml/2 tbsp brown sugar

60ml/4 tbsp peanut butter

30ml/2 tbsp chopped peanuts,
    to garnish

VARIATIONS

*Minced chicken, chopped
prawns (shrimp) and shredded
vegetables can also be used.*

These delicious Vietnamese pork spring rolls, called *cha gio*, are often cooked fresh on stalls at the side of the road for passers-by to snack on.

Spring Rolls
with Satay Sauce

Soak the cellophane noodles for 10 minutes in hot water to cover, then drain well and snip them into short lengths. Mix the noodles, pork, spring onions and beansprouts in a large bowl. Add the coriander, soy sauce, fish sauce and sugar and combine.

Place a spring roll wrapper in front of you with a point facing you. Soften the wrapper by brushing with water. Place a teaspoonful of the filling just below the centre, fold over to the nearest point and roll once. Fold in the sides to enclose, brush the edges with the flour and water, and roll up to seal. Repeat with the remaining wrappers.

Heat the oil for deep-frying in a wok or deep pan to 190°C/375°F. A cube of day-old bread should brown in 30–60 seconds. Carefully transfer the wok or pan to a burner at the table.

To make the satay sauce, pound the chilli and garlic together in a mortar with a pestle. Heat the

oil in a frying pan and fry the chilli paste for a few seconds, then add the coconut milk, sugar and peanut butter. Mix well and simmer for 5 minutes, then pour into a serving bowl and cool. Garnish with chopped peanuts.

Diners fry their spring rolls for 2–3 minutes until golden brown. If you like, wrap each cooked roll in a lettuce leaf with coriander. Serve with the satay sauce for dipping.

INGREDIENTS

Serves 4–6

200g/7oz cod or coley fillet,
* skin removed*
200g/7oz fresh white crab
* meat, or 2 x 120g/4¼oz*
* cans white crab*
* meat, drained*
15ml/1 tbsp red curry paste
10ml/2 tsp Thai fish sauce
115g/4oz green beans,
* finely chopped*
200g/7oz/3½ cups fresh
* breadcrumbs*
vegetable oil, for deep-frying

For the relish

1 small cucumber
2 shallots, finely chopped
2 small red chillies, seeded and
* finely chopped*
25ml/1½ tbsp caster
* (superfine) sugar*
45ml/3 tbsp rice vinegar
15ml/1 tbsp water

COOK'S TIP

When you are keeping oil
fondues hot at the table, it is
best to use a good quality
cook's thermometer, if you have
one, to keep a careful check on
the oil temperature.

These little crab cakes are firm and meaty inside with a crispy coating and distinctive flavours. They are served with a red chilli and cucumber relish.

Crab Cakes
with Thai Cucumber Relish

Remove any remaining bones from the cod or coley, then place in a food processor. Add the crab meat, curry paste, Thai fish sauce and green beans, and pulse until blended. Chill for 1 hour.

With oiled hands, roll small quantities of the crab mixture into about 20 slightly flattened patties. Roll them in the breadcrumbs and place on a serving platter. Chill until ready to serve.

To make the cucumber relish, shred the cucumber on a mandolin or chop it finely. Transfer the cucumber to a serving bowl and add the finely chopped shallots and chillies. Heat the sugar, vinegar and water together in a small pan, stirring occasionally, until the sugar has dissolved, then allow to cool. Pour the cooled liquid over the cucumber mixture, and place in serving saucers.

Heat the oil for deep-frying in a wok or deep pan to 190°C/375°F. If you do not have a cook's thermometer, test by dropping a cube of day-old bread into the hot oil; it should brown in 30–60 seconds. Carefully transfer the wok or pan to a burner at the table.

Each diner drops their own crab cakes into the hot oil and cooks them for 3–5 minutes, or until they are golden brown, and then removes them with chopsticks, tongs or little wire baskets.

Serve with the Thai cucumber relish for dipping.

INGREDIENTS

Serves 4–6

1 medium aubergine (eggplant)

2 red (bell) peppers, seeded

250g/9oz/2¼ cups plain
   (all-purpose) flour, plus extra
   for dusting

4 baby squid, cut into rings

200g/7oz green beans, trimmed

12 mint sprigs

oil, for deep-frying

2 egg yolks

475ml/16fl oz/2 cups iced water

5ml/1 tsp salt

gari (Japanese pickled ginger) or
   grated fresh root ginger,
   and grated daikon or pink
   radishes, to serve

For the dipping sauce

200ml/7fl oz/ scant 1 cup
   water

45ml/3 tbsp mirin or
   sweet sherry

10g/¼oz bonito flakes

45ml/3 tbsp soy sauce

VARIATIONS

• Any seafood is suitable for
cooking in a tempura batter. Try
mussels, clams, prawns (shrimp)
or scallops, or slices of salmon,
cod, tuna or haddock.

• Cauliflower, broccoli,
mangetouts (snow peas) and
green beans work well, too.

Crunchy battered vegetables and crisp squid rings are perfect with a piquant dipping sauce, daikon and pink, pickled ginger in this flavourful Japanese dish.

Tempura

To make the dipping sauce, mix the sauce ingredients together in a pan, bring to the boil and then strain into serving saucers and leave to cool.

Cut the aubergine and peppers into fine julienne strips using a sharp knife or a mandolin. Put the flour for dusting into a plastic bag and add the squid. Shake the bag to coat the squid with a little flour, then place on a serving platter. Repeat with the vegetables and mint.

Heat the oil for deep-frying in a wok or deep pan to 190°C/375°F. If you do not have a cook's thermometer, test by dropping a cube of day-old bread into the hot oil; it should brown in 30–60 seconds. Carefully transfer to a burner at the table.

When ready to eat, beat the egg yolks and the iced water together. Tip in the flour and salt, and stir briefly. It is important that the tempura is lumpy and not mixed to a smooth batter.

Each diner dips the food into the batter and then immediately into the hot oil using chopsticks, long forks or wire baskets. Fry for 2 minutes, or until crisp.

Serve the tempura dipped in the sauce, and accompanied by gari or ginger and daikon or radishes.

COOK'S TIP

If you cannot get hold of bonito flakes, an acceptable substitute would be to use 200ml/7fl oz/ scant 1 cup well-flavoured fish stock instead of the water to make the dipping sauce.

INGREDIENTS

Serves 4–6

4 corn on the cob
450g/1lb potatoes,
peeled and cut into
even-size pieces
2 eggs
dash of Tabasco sauce
5ml/1 tsp Worcestershire
sauce
200g/7oz/2¹/3 cups
desiccated (dry
unsweetened shredded)
coconut
oil, for deep-frying
salt and ground black
pepper
coriander (cilantro) leaves,
to serve

For the salsa

90g/3¹/2oz peeled mango,
finely diced
90g/3¹/2oz peeled papaya,
finely diced
2.5cm/1in piece fresh
root ginger, peeled
and grated
1 shallot or ¹/2 small red
onion, finely chopped
rind and juice of 1 lime

A totally tropical, mellow but vibrant fondue that will perk up even the most tired of palates. Deep-fry coconut corn cakes and serve with piquant salsa.

Caribbean Corn
Cakes with Tropical Salsa

Place the corn and potatoes in a large pan of boiling water and cook for 10–15 minutes, or until the potatoes are just tender. Drain.

Meanwhile, make the salsa by mixing all the ingredients in a bowl. Transfer the salsa to a serving bowl and leave to allow the flavours to blend.

Mash the potatoes and slice the corn kernels from the cobs. Put into a large bowl with the eggs and Tabasco and Worcestershire sauces.

Season with salt and pepper and mix well. Shape the mixture into about 18 small rounds and flatten slightly. Place the coconut on a plate and press each cake into it so that it is coated with the coconut on all sides. Place on a serving platter and chill until ready to serve.

Heat the oil in a wok or deep pan to 190°C/375°F. If you do not have a cook's thermometer, test by dropping a cube of day-old bread into the hot oil; it should brown in 30–60 seconds. Carefully transfer to a burner at the table.

Invite the diners to carefully drop the corn cakes into the hot oil and leave them to cook for 3–5 minutes, or until they are golden brown. Fish the cakes out with wire baskets or tongs and eat topped with the salsa and coriander leaves.

Sweet
fondues

These desserts are quite irresistible. Choose from creamy custard served with mini meringues, blackberry fondue with figs, luscious chocolate fondue or banana fritters with papaya cream.

INGREDIENTS

Serves 4–6

120ml/4fl oz/½ cup milk

300ml/½ pint/1¼ cups single
   (light) cream

1 vanilla pod (bean), split
   lengthways

1 fresh bay leaf

4 egg yolks

50g/2oz/¼ cup vanilla-
   flavoured caster
   (superfine) sugar

200g/7oz/1¾ cups fresh
   summer berries, to serve

For the meringues

115g/4oz/¾ cup fresh
   raspberries

3 egg whites

175g/6oz/scant 1 cup caster
   (superfine) sugar

COOK'S TIPS

- For successful meringues, use
  a large bowl and make sure
  that both the bowl and whisk
  are scrupulously clean.
- Whisk the egg whites until
  they are very stiff before
  adding the sugar.
- When making the crème
  anglaise cook the eggs slowly
  and gently or they will curdle.
  Patience will be rewarded with
  a smooth, thickened custard.

**Dainty meringues and fresh berries are
dipped into a creamy egg custard,
making this luscious fondue dessert a
wonderful finale to a summer meal.**

Crème Anglaise
with Raspberry Meringues

First make the meringues. Preheat the oven to 120°C/250°F/Gas ½ and line two baking trays with baking parchment. Place the raspberries in a food processor or blender and blend to a purée, then strain through a sieve. Whisk the egg whites until they hold stiff peaks. Add half the sugar, a tablespoonful at a time, whisking between each addition until you have a light, firm and glossy meringue. Fold in the remaining sugar.

Place small heaps of the meringue (about two teaspoonfuls) well apart on the baking trays, and make a slight hollow in the centre of each with the back of a wet teaspoon. Place a teaspoonful of the raspberry purée into the hollow of each and then top with a little more meringue.

Bake the meringues for 1½ hours, or until crisp, yet still slightly soft in the centre.

Heat the milk and cream in a pan with the vanilla pod and bay leaf until almost boiling. Whisk the egg yolks and sugar together in a large bowl until pale and creamy, then whisk in the hot milk and cream. Return to a low heat and stir constantly until thickened.

Transfer to a fondue pot on a burner at the table. Keep the crème anglaise warm over a very low heat, and serve it with the raspberry meringues and berries for dipping.

INGREDIENTS

Serves 4–6

200g/7oz dark (bittersweet)
   chocolate
75ml/2¹/₂fl oz/¹/₃ cup strong
   black coffee
75g/3oz/scant ¹/₃ cup soft light
   brown sugar
120ml/4fl oz/¹/₂ cup double
   (heavy) cream
small, firm scoops of vanilla
   ice cream decorated with
   crystallized (candied) violets,
   to serve

For the poached pears

juice of 1 lemon
90g/3¹/₂oz/¹/₂ cup vanilla
   caster (superfine) sugar
1–2 fresh rosemary sprigs
12–18 small pears, or 4–6
   large pears

COOK'S TIPS

• *To make mini ice-cream balls,*
  use a melon baller instead of
  an ice cream scoop. Dip the
  melon baller in warm water
  between scoops.
• *Ensure that the ice-cream*
  balls are very firm before
  serving: arrange them on a
  metal tray as you scoop them
  and then refreeze the balls for
  at least an hour.

**Rosemary and vanilla-scented pears
and scoops of daintily decorated ice
cream are dipped into a rich chocolate
fondue for this splendid dessert.**

Bitter Chocolate
Fondue with Poached Pears

To make the poached pears, put the lemon juice, sugar, rosemary sprigs and 300ml/½ pint/1¼ cups water in a pan large enough to accommodate the pears all in one layer. Bring to the boil, stirring occasionally, to ensure that the sugar dissolves in the water.

Peel the pears, and halve the large ones, if using, but leave the stalks intact. Add to the boiling syrup and spoon over to cover.

Cook for 5–10 minutes, depending on the size and ripeness of the pears, spooning the syrup over them and turning them frequently, until they are only just tender. Transfer the pears to a serving plate, then remove the rosemary sprigs from the syrup. Pull off about 15–30ml/1–2 tbsp of the rosemary leaves and stir them into the syrup and then leave to cool.

Break the chocolate into pieces and place in a heatproof bowl over a pan of barely simmering water. Add the coffee and sugar and heat, without stirring, until the chocolate is melted. Stir in the cream and heat gently. Transfer the hot fondue to a fondue pot and place on a burner set at a low heat at the table.

Serve the pears and syrup together with the decorated vanilla ice cream to dip into the hot chocolate fondue.

INGREDIENTS

Serves 4–6

800g/1¾lb/7 cups blackberries

juice of 2 lemons

175g/6oz/scant 1 cup caster
(superfine) sugar

300ml/½ pint/1¼ cups
Zinfandel rosé wine

30ml/2 tbsp cornflour
(cornstarch) blended to
a paste with about
30ml/2 tbsp water

105ml/7 tbsp crème de mûre
or crème de cassis

15ml/1 tbsp chopped
fresh mint

16 ripe, fresh figs, quartered

For the pastries

plain (all-purpose) flour and
icing (confectioners') sugar,
for dusting and rolling

375g/13oz puff pastry, thawed
if frozen

275g/10oz white marzipan

caster (superfine) sugar,
for dusting

VARIATION

*Cubes of sweet breads such as
brioche or panettone would be
perfect with this fondue, as
would crunchy Italian cookies
such as cantucci or biscotti.*

Spiral-shaped, crisp marzipan pastries and sweet fresh figs are wonderful dipped into a lemon-and-mint-scented hot blackberry-and-wine fondue. Make this in late summer or early autumn when blackberries are plentiful.

Blackberry Fondue with Figs and Frangipane Pastries

To make the pastries, preheat the oven to 180°C/350°F/Gas 4, line a baking sheet with baking parchment, and dust a work surface with flour. Roll out the pastry to a 30 x 20cm/12 x 8in rectangle, then dust the work surface with icing sugar and roll out the marzipan to the same size.

Place the marzipan on top of the pastry, then roll both together to make a long sausage shape. Cut crossways into 1cm/½in slices and arrange on the prepared baking sheet. Bake for 15 minutes, or until puffed and tinged golden brown. Transfer to a cooling rack, and dust with caster sugar.

Blend the blackberries in a food processor with the lemon juice, then press through a sieve into a pan. Add the sugar and wine and bring to the boil, then simmer for 20 minutes, skimming off any scum that rises to the top. Stir in the blended cornflour and cook, stirring, until thickened. Add the liqueur.

Transfer to a fondue pot, add the mint, and place on a burner at the table. Serve with the pastries and figs.

INGREDIENTS

Serves 4–6

oil, for deep-frying
900g/2lb bananas
juice of 1 lime
lime wedges and caster
    (superfine) sugar, to serve

For the batter

175ml/6fl oz/³⁄4 cup water
150g/5oz/1¹⁄4 cups plain
    (all-purpose) flour
115g/4oz/1¹⁄3 cups desiccated
    (dry unsweetened
    shredded) coconut
2.5ml/¹⁄2 tsp salt
75g/3oz/6 tbsp caster
    (superfine) sugar
1 egg, beaten

For the papaya cream

2 papayas, quartered, seeded
    and skinned
juice of 1 lime
300ml/¹⁄2 pint/1¹⁄4 cups
    double (heavy) cream
50g/2oz/¹⁄2 cup icing
    (confectioners') sugar, sieved

Bananas, dipped in coconut batter, are fried at the table until soft inside and crisp outside. A lime-flavoured papaya cream makes an exotic dip.

Banana Fritters with Papaya Cream

To make the batter, put all the batter ingredients in a bowl and mix together well using a wooden spoon. Leave to rest in a cool place for 20 minutes, then transfer the mixture to a serving bowl.

To make the papaya cream, put the papayas and the lime juice in a food processor or blender and process to a purée. Whip the cream until just beginning to thicken, then fold in the papaya purée and sugar. Spoon into serving dishes and chill.

Heat the oil for deep-frying in a wok or deep pan to 190°C/375°F. If you do not have a cook's thermometer, test by dropping a cube of day-old bread into the hot oil; it should brown in 30–60 seconds. Transfer the wok or pan to a burner at the table.

Peel the bananas, cut each in half lengthways, and then cut each half crossways into two slices about 7.5cm/3in long. Squeeze over the lime juice to prevent them discolouring, then transfer to a serving platter.

Each diner makes his or her own fritters by first dipping the banana slices in the batter to coat and then deep-frying them for about 30 seconds, or until golden and crispy. Drain the fritters on kitchen paper, squeeze over some lime juice and sprinkle with caster sugar, then dip into the papaya cream and eat.

Index

AUG 2 1 2008